# JUST A MOMENT, LORD

# JUST A MOMENT, LORD

by

FLORA LARSSON

**HODDER AND STOUGHTON**
LONDON SYDNEY AUCKLAND TORONTO

# CONTENTS

## GOOD DAYS AND BAD

## THE MOTLEY CROWD WITHIN

# OTHERS

# TOO SMALL A SAINT

# WITH CLEARER SIGHT

## LISTEN, LORD

## LEARNING IN GOD'S SCHOOL

# CONTENTS

## UNKNOWN TOMORROWS

# GOOD DAYS AND BAD

# My heart sings

Today my heart sings, Lord;
Everything within me rejoices.

> Joy bubbles up in my soul,
> overflows and cascades like a stream leaping all
>     barriers;
> the joy of knowing You,
> the joy of union with You.

One with You, Creator of the world,
      and my Creator,
one with You, Saviour of the world,
      and my Saviour.
One with You, Spirit of the eternal God,
      and my God,
one with You, almighty King of kings
      and my Lord and King.

> Joy, joy at the heart of living,
> joy in doing, joy in being;

sing for joy, my heart,
for sheer joy, my soul.

The joy of loving You,
the joy of following You,
the joy of serving You;
all the way 'long it is glory.

Today my heart sings, Lord;
everything within me rejoices,
joy bubbles up in my soul,
glory . . . glory!

# Where are You?

MASTER, WHERE ARE YOU?
Yesterday I knew.
Yesterday I rejoiced in Your love;
Your presence enhanced each task;
Your comfort filled my heart.

Today, where are You?
Withdrawn?
Why, Lord?

Today is empty.
>> Today has no joys;
>> today has no wings;
>> today has no glad future;
All is drear, meaningless.
>> Why, Lord?

Has the veil of my flesh thickened so as to shut You out?
Have the shutters of my mind snapped together?
Have I carelessly left the blinds drawn on the windows
>> of my soul?

Show me, Master, if the fault is mine.
Help me to put it right,
and, if it is simply a weakness of the earthen vessel that
>> bears Your likeness without Your power,
help me still to believe in You;
to hold on in trust until my soul revives.

For I'm lonely without You, Lord,
and without You I cannot live.

# Courage to live

LORD, GIVE ME COURAGE TO LIVE!
A cheerful courage, Master, if that might be.
Let me wear a smile even when my heart trembles;
let laughter-lines form round my eyes,
and let me hold my chin up
and go forward.

Lord, give me courage to live!
A grim, unsmiling courage, if need be.
Courage to face the empty days,
      unfulfilled hopes,
      black hours,
      defeats, maybe;
A hard, defiant courage, that will hang on
      until things are better.
      Grant me that, Lord.

Master, give me courage to live!
Your servant Sangster wrote that 'in the dark,
      brave souls hold on to the skirts of God'.
Give me courage like that, Lord,
      clinging courage, desperate courage,
      that will not let You go.
If feeling goes, if faith goes, if fortitude fails,
      let me just hold on,

14

clinging to You,
knowing that You are there,
counting on You to see me through.


# An awful day


TODAY, LORD, HAS BEEN AWFUL!
    It started badly.
Imps of depression sat on the bedposts
    waiting for me to wake,
    ready to pounce on me,
    to harry me
    and fill me with their gloom.

My head ached, my nerves were edgy
    and I felt irritable.

And then it rained . . .
not a decent sort of rain, soon over and done with,
but a penetrating, miserable, drooling kind of rain
that wet-blanketed soul as well as body.

There are days like that, Master.
Days when life is heavy, boring, meaningless;
days when no ray pierces the inward gloom,
    just plain bad days.

What is Your recipe for such hours, Lord?
I am reminded of some words which were often on Your
       lips:
    'Take heart!'
They must have comforted Your followers many times.
You used them when they were startled,
      when they had lost their nerve,
      when they needed encouragement.

I need encouragement, Master,
so I quieten my mind and wait to hear You say:
    'Take heart!'
Thank You, Lord.


# My mind races

I CAN'T BE STILL, LORD, AS YOU COMMAND.
      My body is immobile,
      but my mind races;
      leaps from one subject to another;
      flies off at a tangent.

In the distance I hear the soft chiming of a church clock.
Outside my window seagulls ride on the wind,
the friendly sparrows enjoy a morning chat.
A neighbour waters her flowers.

16

And yet my mind races on though my body remains
    relaxed.
    The past, the present, the future.
    What I have done,
    should have done,
    still have to do.

Things press upon my mind from all directions.
    I feel chased,
    burdened,
    overwhelmed.

How do I find Your peace, Lord?
    Peace within me,
    a quiet mind,
    a tranquil heart.
These are what I need,
and these are what You have promised.

    Make me receptive, Master.
    Let me feel Your peace flowing into my mind,
    stilling the inward storms,
    calming and quieting,
    soothing and strengthening.
    Just now, Lord, now.

# A perfect day

I WANT TO THANK YOU FOR A PERFECT DAY, LORD.
Everything has gone right,
every single little thing, as well as the big things.
There was sunshine this morning, with tiny white clouds
          sailing across the blue heavens,
the dewy flowers laughed at me as I walked down the
          garden path,
and roses wafted their delicious scent in my direction.


Heavenly Father, when You planned Your world,
          why did You make it so breathtakingly beautiful?
          It hurts, Lord,
          so much beauty hurts.
          It makes a pain inside that is a pain of joy,
          a quivering, glowing, lovely little pain
          that bursts into the heart and fills it.


I hardly dare to live in Your world when You show its
          splendours.
          It is too big for me,
          too marvellous.
But into the small world of my home I fit.
There I can be myself, and the hours alone are not hours
          of loneliness,
          except at times.

Today, though, joy has filled my heart.
    African violets nodded to me from the window sill,
    and the radio played such happy tunes that I
      danced
    across the floor as I dusted,
    which resulted in very skimpy dusting, Lord.
    But You understand, don't You?

I was too happy to bother about such trifles as specks of
      dust,
    so thank You.
Thank You a thousand times for this happy day.
    Good night.

# Mist on the hills

MIST ON THE HILLS!
Fog on the roads,
The outlook gloomy with a sense of unreality.
An uncomfortable feeling of being choked,
enclosed by a stifling grey blanket.

Teach me to live on my memories, Lord.
    To picture the distant mountain,
    the sunlight glinting on the river,
    patterned by the wake of small boats.

The unseen is there, is real and living!
Let me rejoice in that knowledge and await;
    clarity of vision will return.

So too, Lord, let it be in my spiritual life.
    When clouds imprison me
    and faith is dulled;
    when love is cold
    and truth seems dead.

Then let me call to mind Your former graciousness.
    Moments when my heart responded,
    when my soul rejoiced in Your presence,
    my faith shone bright and firm.

The unseen is there, is real and living!
Let me rejoice in that knowledge and await;
    clarity of vision will return.

# Yesterday

YESTERDAY IS AN OLD GARMENT, LORD,
    creased, stained and threadbare.
    Help me to throw it off,
    casting it into the coffers of the past,
    done with, laid aside and forgotten.

Let me not walk in my yesterdays;
      not live again the used-up hours,
      regretting the misspent moments,
      brooding over the rebuffs,
      fingering the tattered glory-rags,
      clutching them close to my eager breast.

Today is new, fresh from Your hands,
      glowing with promise of fulfilment,
      full of opportunities,
      of duties,
      of joys;
      with perhaps a tinge of sorrow.

Let me wear 'today' hopefully,
      grateful that it is mine,
      glad to face its challenge,
      using unstintingly
      each moment as it comes.

For tonight, Master, tonight I must lay it off,
      an old garment,
      creased, stained and threadbare,
      casting it into the coffers of the past,
      done with, laid aside and forgotten.

# THE MOTLEY CROWD
## WITHIN

# Saint in embryo

There's a queer fellow lives within me,
      Master.
    He calls himself 'Saint in Embryo'.
How much saint there is about him, I don't know,
but he sure is embryonic.
Sometimes I hardly know that he exists.
    Saint in Embryo leads a hard life, Lord.
    Everything is against him.
    He always has to row against the tide
    and battle with contrary winds.


He will insist on lugging that over-polished halo with him,
    and when he has said something good, really good,
    or done something fine, really fine,
    instead of leaving matters there
    and slipping quietly away,
He spoils things by putting on his old halo,
    which sits at a rakish angle,
    being too big for him.

Lord, he makes himself ridiculous.
Why can't he learn to do good stealthily,
to be good without being puffed up with pride?

I've remonstrated with him about that halo, Master,
      but he says he is forced to wear it
      or people won't know he's trying to be a saint.

When I pointed out that it didn't matter what others
      thought
      but only what You thought
      he looked a bit ashamed
      and tried to hide his halo behind his back.

This 'Saint in Embryo' has got a lot to learn, Master.
Will You take him in hand and train him?

# Big me

TODAY, LORD, HAS BEEN A BAD DAY.
Big Me obscured my vision.
Not only my vision of other people and their interests,
that would have been bad enough,
but worse, Master.
Big Me obscured my vision of You.

This bloated, arrogant Self took the upper hand,
    and I let him do it;
    not with absolute approval,
    but yet with my consent.
Big Me had had a hard day,
he had been ignored, squashed, belittled . . .

    Big Me was furious
    and rampant,
    on the war path.
And Lord, He blotted You out,
    with his swollen self-importance
    he blurred the outlines of Your face.

I sat in a sacred service.
One of Your servants was proclaiming the rich mercies of
    Your grace;
    I only heard Big Me's complaints.
The congregation sang the triumphs of Your love;
    Big Me drowned their praise with his raucous
    voice.
Tender verses from Your Book were read;
    Big Me was unmoved.

What can I do, Master, when Big Me takes the reins?
Can You deliver me from his dominance?

# Self-pity

LORD, THERE'S SOMEONE LURKING WITHIN ME:
Shrouded and gloomy she goes her way
    with downcast eyes,
    dragging steps,
    and doleful mien.

She's the shadow of a better me.
She's something good gone sour,
self-replete and self-stifled.

To hear her talk is a revelation;
no one ever had it so bad.
Her setbacks are unrivalled,
her problems mountain-high.
Turned in upon herself she mopes and broods,
    sobs and sighs;
    poor me . . . poor me . . .
    poor miserable me!

Out upon you, traitor, I cry:
I'll have none of your mournful dirges . . .
away with you from my house of life!

Master, give me courage to throw her out:
let me get rid of her once and for all,
and bar the door against her.

Help me to bear bravely my own share of life's burdens;
help me to find others who also suffer
    and try to bring them comfort.
Let me take another's hand in mine and say:
      Courage! the storm will pass;
      look up, day will soon dawn.


Lord, save me from self-pity.


# Touchy


MASTER, MAY I INTRODUCE TOUCHY?
I'm not exactly proud of him, I can assure You.
Touchy has lived with me since I was a teenager;
    an unwelcome but most persistent lodger,
      who takes upon himself an old lodger's privilege
    of making himself at home
    and trying to rule.


Touchy has invisible tentacles that stick out in all
      directions,
with the inevitable result that he's always getting hurt:
    hurt in feelings,
    hurt in his affections,
    hurt in his self-esteem.

He takes offence at the most innocent remark.
He regards every suggestion as a personal affront,
and any criticism as a direct attack.

Lord, it's very unpleasant to live with Touchy.
       I've tried turning him out many times,
       but before I've shut the door on him
       he jumps in through the window.
       He seems to think he belongs.

I've tried reasoning with him and he says:
       'But I'm so sensitive. You don't understand.'
I've tried laughing at him
       but tears well up in his eyes and he sobs.
I've toughened him up a bit by ignoring him,
but what a relief it would be
       to get rid of him for ever.

Could you fill me with more of Your spirit, Lord,
so that Touchy would be squeezed right out?

# Great-aunt Maria

GREAT-AUNT MARIA IS A BIG TRIAL TO ME, LORD.
Why need she poke her long nose into everything?
Why should her shadow darken my existence?

30

Breathing with every breath I draw,
inevitably and irrevocably a part of me,
linking me up in the chain of the generations;
quirks, foibles, pet aversions, animosities . . .
All these are Great-aunt Maria flowing in my veins.

Great-aunt Maria didn't like spiders,
therefore I do not like spiders,
and my daughter doesn't like spiders;
so on, ad infinitum.

But that is quite a harmless idiosyncrasy.
There are other things, much more serious:
tendencies,
reactions,
whims and fears,
strong antipathies,
all of them part of my built-in mechanism;
all of them influencing my life,
colouring my thoughts,
and affecting my service for You, Master.

Lord, must Great-aunt Maria live with me to the end of
my days?
Must I be me and yet her all my life through?
Can I never shake off her dominance?

# Braggart

BRAGGART REALLY IS A PEST, MASTER,
He makes me sick when he takes over;
boasting, boosting, embroidering.
     What he is,
     what he's done,
     what he's going to do.
Usch! I'm disgusted with him.

Of course, I know why he does it.
Even a child has that much psychology.
He does it because he feels inferior.

But why should he feel inferior,
just because he isn't like someone else?

Lord, if Braggart would only be himself,
his very ordinary but his best self,
all would be well.

You have made us all different,
     because You want it that way, Lord.
We don't need to eat our hearts out
     because we can't sing like A,
     or write like B,
     or talk like C.

I'm always telling Braggart this,
    And basically I think he understands,
but he forgets, Master. And then he starts to brag.
Please forgive him, Lord.
He's not a bad fellow at heart,
but I find it a bit trying at times to co-exist with him.


# An old fogey


IT'S NOT VERY NICE TO BE AN OLD FOGEY, LORD.
I don't feel an old fogey,
    even if I might look one.
Inside one doesn't feel old,
it's the outside that decays so quickly.


    Lined face,
    sagging muscles,
    greying hair
And young folk class you as an old fogey,
thinking that you have forgotten what it is to be young.


    They little know the gay dialogues,
    the continued questings,
    the voiceless yearnings
    that go on under that ageing exterior.

You were never old, Master.
You died in young manhood,
so You never felt the slackening of the life-lines as the
       years mounted.
But Your mother stood near the Cross, with tired face
       and greying hair.

    And You loved her,
    cared for her,
    provided for her.
So You will be compassionate with those of us termed 'old
      fogies', won't You?

Even if we are slow on the up-take . . .
for the will to do still exists when the power to do departs.
The tenant remains youthful while the house decays.

It is Your own law, Master,
and You know best.

# Niggard

WHAT A MEAN OLD FELLOW NIGGARD IS, MASTER!
I don't mean only with money, though that is included,
for he was brought up to be careful
    and to count his pennies.

You taught that it is better to give than to get, Lord,
    but Niggard won't believe that,
    or at any rate he won't practise it.
He says that what you keep you have,
and what you give away you lose.
    That is why he is so mean.

But money is not his biggest weakness.
His worst fault is that he is so mean with appreciation.
How a compliment sticks in his throat!
To ask him to say 'Well done' to another
    would be to risk him choking over the words.

How can I get him to be more generous?
    To be quick to say a kindly word,
    to jump at the chance to congratulate,
    to encourage when the going is hard,
    to share another's joy.

I shall have to insist, Lord,
stand over him and say: 'Smile!'
Take him by the neck and force the issue.

I don't want this old Niggard within me, Master.
Teach me how to outwit him,
to make life so uncomfortable for him
    that he will quit for good.

# In a quandary

LORD, I'M IN A QUANDARY.
     What shall I do?
Various voices rise within me and give me counsel,
     but their advice is contrary
     and I am left perplexed, bewildered.


Great-aunt Maria, old suffragette that she is,
     tells me to stand no nonsense,
     put my foot down firmly,
     let them know who they're dealing with.


Big Me sides with her.
     Those two are usually allies
     when it suits their own interests.
He speaks very forcibly and even eloquently,
     pointing out the reasonableness of my objections.
     'You have to stand up for your rights,
     otherwise people won't respect you.
     They'll walk on you,
     using you as a doormat.'


Touchy seems very upset, but he snivels so much
     I can't understand what he's trying to say.

Then 'Saint in Embryo' breaks in.
    Quietly, persuasively,
    he argues the other side,
    and advises a peaceful, even a pleasant approach.

So what shall I do, Lord? I'm pulled in different direc-
        tions.
I want to do what is right,
    not necessarily in other people's view.

Please, Master, show me what is best,
        and give me the courage to do it.

# OTHERS

# My enemy

MASTER, YOU SAID SOME HARD THINGS.
You said: 'Love your enemies.'
At first sight it does not look so difficult,
as long as I think of my enemies as out there,
      far, far away.

In jungles where matted grasses block the paths,
in hot, barren deserts where goat-skin tents sprawl like
      overgrown mushrooms close to the baked ground,
in the cold north and southlands where they fight blizzards
      through the long, dark winters;
in great noisy cities where they drive their cars on the
      wrong side of the road.

Enemies?
They are people with features other than my own,
      neither better nor worse,
      just otherwise.
They are people with skins unlike my own,
      neither better nor worse,
      just different.

They are people with languages I can't understand,
       strange to my ears.

Those imaginary enemies that I shall never see or know,
       those I can think kindly of,
       those I can pray for,
       those I can love.

But, Lord, it is my enemy next door that troubles me.
       Her children pick my flowers,
       her dog dirties my front path,
       her drab washing flaps uglily when I have visitors;
       she is not tidy in her dress and sometimes – this is
       just between You and me, Lord – she smells.

Lord, do You really expect me to love *her*?
I'm quite prepared to go half-way,
       to come to some arrangement with her,
       so that we can co-exist in a state of armed neutrality
       over the garden fence.

But *love* her?
Lord, You ask the impossible.
I can't do it.
Will You help me by showing me how to achieve the
       impossible?

# The beatnik

LORD, I'VE SEEN ONE OF THOSE STRANGE CREATURES,
    A beatnik.
From behind the window pane I could watch him at
        leisure.
    He drifted by,
    dirty, unkempt,
    slovenly and down at heel,
    a human wreck,
    but a young wreck.

Master, what would You have said to such a one
        had You met him on the Galilean shore?
You met the sick, the sad, the suffering, the needy,
        but did You meet a beatnik?

I remember, you once met an elegant young man
        and how Your heart went out to him.
What do You feel toward a beatnik?
        Contempt or compassion?
        Scorn or love?
Would the lines of Your face harden or grow tender?
What would Your eyes reveal?
I am certain that they would challenge him,
would pierce the dirty, careless crust
        To find the spark of manhood within.

You would stretch out Your hand in friendship,
      speak cheerily to him,
      sit down with him and chat.
      He would talk to You
      and You would listen.

Then You would talk, Master, You who hold the keys of
      the hearts of men;
You would know how to win him away from himself.
When he rose there would be a new light in his eyes,
      a firmness in his step,
For You would have given his life new meaning.

O Master, if only I could learn from You
      how to win the souls of men,
      beatniks, mods and rockers and others.
      Won't You teach me Your secret?

# About Mrs. Fell

I'D LIKE TO TALK TO YOU ABOUT MRS. FELL, LORD.
To say that she and I are not on the same wavelength
      is putting it too mildly;
We are directly antagonistic and for no known reason.
      She is a most excellent woman.

The perfect wife mentioned in Your Book couldn't hold
      a candle to her;
      yet while I admire her
      I dislike her.
      Am I simply jealous of her
      because her virtues show up my shortcomings?

I want to love Mrs. Fell.
No! that's not exactly the truth, Master.
I *don't* want to love Mrs. Fell!
Very definitely not.
I must put my desire in another form:
I want You to make me love her.
No! that's not true either.
I must find another formula.

I'd like You to take from me that which makes me dislike
      her.
(I'd like You to do a bit of work on her too,
      for I'm sure she heartily dislikes me.)
But if You would just show me where the fault lies in me,
that would be the beginning of a new approach;
and a new approach might lead to better understanding,
and better understanding to mutual regard.

I'm sorry to give You all this trouble, Lord.
I ought to have brought this matter to You long ago.
      Forgive my tardiness.
In Your goodness help me to get straight on this point,
then there will be one less problem in my life.

# Some people are impossible

SOME PEOPLE ARE IMPOSSIBLE, LORD.
They go around wearing brooches engraved 'Others First'.
How do You feel about that, Master?

Aren't they going a bit too far?
      Further than You intended?
      Further than You commanded?

I know Your words quite well and find them
      uncomfortable to live with.

You said: 'Love your neighbour as yourself' –
      not better than yourself
      or worse than yourself,
      but as much as yourself.
And that is hard enough in all conscience.

If that is what You want, Master,
      why did You make me as I am?
For I very definitely love myself more than any other.
      It's instinctive.
      It's natural.

I know, of course, that You want us to live by grace
      rather than by nature.

46

But, Lord, it's going to take an awful lot of grace
     to change the natural man.


Is Your supply unlimited, Master?
     For it will need to be
Just to make this one self-lover into an other-lover.


# Someone's pet corn

TODAY I TROD ON SOMEONE'S PET CORN, MASTER,
Hard, ruthlessly but unintentionally.
How was I to know, Lord, that just that subject was his
     sore point?
     I had never seen the man before.
     Why should a few innocent remarks awake such
     anger?


I tried to think of the soft answer that might turn away his
     wrath,
but, Lord, You know I am not nimble-witted in such
     matters.
The gracious and disarming reply does not rise naturally
     and quickly within me.
So I bowed my head and let the storm pass over.

I felt sorry afterward, Lord,
for he was worried,
tense, overburdened, nervy and explosive,
ready-laid kindling for any stray spark.
And I struck the match which made him flare.

Somewhere there must have been a fire extinguisher,
but my eyes couldn't see it,
my hands couldn't grasp it.
Perhaps I really didn't look for it hard enough . . .
and the mischief was done.

I'm sorry, Lord.
Sorry for that servant of Yours whose nerves were
on edge,
Sorry that I was the stumbling-block over which
he tripped.
Please, dear Lord, would You bless him just now.
Let him forget this incident, as I will try to forget it.
Make us both just a little wiser next time we meet,
and let us meet as friends.

# A rebuke

LORD, I HAVE RECEIVED A REBUKE.
  Not from You, Master,
  although I might well deserve it.
  But from a young man.
  He said nothing to me;
  he did nothing to me;
  but I saw him,
  and seeing, I was humbled
  and contrite.

He sat in a restaurant, his plate before him.
  He ate like a dog, Master,
  just like a dog.
  Lapping up ice-cream with his lips and tongue
  direct from the plate.

My inward reaction was swift . . . and unforgivable.
  Modern youth!
  What new monstrosity will they invent?
And then I watched and understood.

His twisted arms hung uselessly on his knees.
  He was a cripple,
  a young cripple;
  going through life with a terrible defect.

And in my heart I had blamed him,
    blamed him for unseemly behaviour,
    this fine, brave lad,
    suffering people's pitying gaze
    each day of his life;
    living differently because he must;
    each day a new crucifixion.


Forgive me, Master,
I take this rebuke as from You.
Help me not to judge without knowing,
    not to jump to conclusions,
    not to condemn without evidence,
    nor to hurt any of my fellow men needlessly,
    remembering that to know all is to forgive all.

# A simple sum

THAT WAS A SIMPLE SUM YOU SET PETER, MASTER.
Seventy times seven . . .
Any child could give the answer:
    four hundred and ninety.
But to forgive a man four hundred and ninety times
    is a hard task;
    infinitely hard.

It goes against the grain,
like so many other of Your commands.

What that person did against me was not so serious,
      but it stung my pride,
      it wounded my self-esteem.
If I've forgiven her once, I've forgiven her a dozen times,
      for there's the rub, Master!

It's not four hundred and ninety separate faults that I
      need Your help to forgive,
I have to keep on forgiving her for the same old fault,
      way back in the past,
      done with long ago.
      I'm ashamed to own it, Lord,
      but You know it's true,
      so why should I try to hide it.

Even when I want to forgive, my forgiveness is not
      complete.
      Deep down within me a memory lies buried.
      Association wakes it to life;
      the reawakening brings fresh resentment;
      and I have to seek Your grace to forgive again.

O Master, if You treated me like that,
      where should I be?
You forgive and forget once and for all.
My sins are sunk in the bottomless sea of Your mercy and
      love.

Dig deep, Lord, deep into the depths of my heart,
Down where these old sores lie festering.
>Pour in Your healing love,
>teach me to forgive
>as You forgive me,
>once and for all.

# Annabella Jones

LORD, WHAT CAN I DO ABOUT ANNABELLA JONES?
How I feel about her can hardly have escaped Your
>notice,
>for she calls out the worst in me.

At sight of her I sprout prickles all over,
>feel my nerves on edge
>and my temper rising.

If You ask me to define my objections, I can't do it.
>Everything about her irritates me.
>To start with, her name!
I know she isn't responsible for what her parents called
>her,
but that knowledge doesn't change my feelings
>which are quite unreasonable.
No one has the right to tack a name like Annabella
>on to plain Jones.

It isn't my business, I know, Master,
but it annoys me all the same.
What can I do about it?

Lord, I come to You,
all hot and bothered and unreasonable.
Calm me down, quieten me, make me sensible.
Teach me not to get upset over small matters.
Don't let a person's name come between us,
      nor the colour of her hair,
      Nor the way she walks
      or how she talks.

Make me a better mixer with all kinds of people, Lord.
      Let me accept them for what they are,
      try to find their good points
      and overlook the rest.

# People lean on me

PEOPLE LEAN ON ME, MASTER.
      Lean heavily,
And I don't want to be leaned on.
I myself want to lean on someone else
      for support,
      for comfort,

for understanding,
for approval.

So what am I to do, Lord, when people lean on me
for sympathy,
for strength,
for love,
for prayers?

One has to be strong to be leaned on
and I am not strong, Master,
not in myself.
I need a new infusion of Your power.

Can You so undergird and stabilise me
that I can bear up against these leanings
and offer myself as a wall of strength
to those with trembling limbs?

Will You take away my own desire
to lean on others,
And teach me to lean only on You, dear Lord?
In that way I could be strong,
for Your strength and courage would flow into my heart
and through me out to others.
Then when they leaned on me
I should not fail them,
for I should be leaning hard on You.

# TOO SMALL A SAINT

# Not good enough

MASTER, I FEEL YOUR CENSURE OVER MY LIFE:
    good, but not good enough,
    warm, but not glowing,
    shallow instead of deep,
    casual instead of committed,
    indifferent instead of involved,
    soft instead of sturdy.


What can I do about it, Lord?
What is wrong?


Does self sit too securely in the saddle?
Is it body-tiredness, mental strain,
    or has it a deeper cause?
Is it the looseness of a rubber band at rest,
    or of one that has lost its stretch?
Is it the long slow decline into the valley of age?
    Passing or permanent?

You see, Lord, what a lot of questions I ask You,
and yet I don't really need any answers.
All I require is new contact with You,
      a quickening,
      a refreshing,
      a renewal.
Then I shall be able to continue.

Meet with me, Master, just now,
stretch out Your hand and I will stretch out mine . . .
There !
now I can go on.

# Hedges

I SAW IT SO CLEARLY, LORD,
Through the words of one of Your servants.

I have built hedges around my life
      without realising it.
      Higher and higher they have grown
      without my knowledge.

These hedges have shut others out
      and myself in.
It was comfortable so, comfortable and cosy.

Less demanded of me,
less expected of me,
only myself to consider.

I have hedged about my time. *My* time!
Did I create time to be my own?
Have I sovereign right to twenty-four hours a day?
Is not each hour a token of Your grace?

I have hedged about my leisure.
My free time is my own, I have said,
and I have miserly gloated over it,
resenting any encroachment upon it.

I have hedged about my love.
These, and these only, I care for,
my nearest, my dearest, my friends,
all precious because they are *mine*.

Forgive me, Lord. Forgive my selfish living,
my self-centredness
my disregard of others.
Help me to tear down the high hedges I have built
and in their place to plan an open garden.
Then I can look out
and others can look in
and we shall be drawn nearer to one another.

# The wheel of duty

I'M BOUND TO THE WHEEL OF DUTY, MASTER;
It whirls round, carrying me in its dizzy turnings.
    I long at times for freedom but must go on.
    I say, 'Stop', but it doesn't stop.
    I say, 'Can't' . . .
    but I find I can because I must.


Lord, my hands hold precious things;
eternal truths are on my lips,
very often on my lips;
    and I'm afraid.


    Afraid of becoming mechanical.
    Afraid of talking for the sake of talking,
    repeating a lesson well learned.
    Playing a part
    with my thoughts elsewhere,
    my interest elsewhere.


Don't let me become a machine, Lord,
    however well adapted,
    however effective,
    however productive.

Help me to give myself with my message,
  some of myself in everything I do:
And when pressure is heavy and the programme packed,
  come to me with some special grace.


  Let me link on to Your strength,
  let me rest in Your love,
  let me remain a tool in Your hands
  and not become a self-propelling gadget.


Lord, I'm afraid: afraid of becoming a machine.
  Only You can help me.
  Come to me now.
  Touch me into new awareness of Your presence;
  let me remain a channel of Your love,
  an instrument for Your use,
  not a robot.


# The hydra-headed monster


YOU SAID SOME STRANGE THINGS, MASTER,
  things that I often ponder.
You said that a man must deny himself
  if he would follow You.

But self has more lives than any cat!
That is what experience has taught me, Lord.
It is a hydra-headed monster,
making a resolute come-back from every knock-out blow.

Talk of split personality!
  We're all split into fractions,
  pulled in several directions at once.

Your task is to integrate us, Lord,
  to make of many bits a whole,
  and a decent whole;
Cementing the various parts by one dominant purpose;
  to live according to Your laws and plans
  with self as obedient servant.

Self as servant and not as master?
  Try it out and see.
Just put the old fellow off his throne
and You'll have a lot of trouble on Your hands.

Master, this is going to be a daily battle,
a stand-up fight to the death.
Help me not to weary of it,
not to tire of slaying the foe within,
for I want to follow You.

# You took me too seriously

YOU TOOK ME TOO SERIOUSLY, LORD.
When I said I would go anywhere for You,
I didn't mean a place like Blackpoint.
      It's obvious that I couldn't go there.
      You understand that, don't You?
      The climate is damp,
      so I might get rheumatism;
      then the houses are built in long rows,
      long, monotonous rows,
      and living under those circumstances
      might cramp my individualistic style.

I am quite willing to go anywhere for You, Master,
      with certain reservations.
I just want this to be clear between ourselves
so that You don't ask me to do anything that is
      beyond my normal capacity,
      contrary to my usual custom,
      or infringing on my personal rights.

Then when I said I would give You my all,
      it was just a figure of speech.
      I trust You understand it like that.
      It was poetic language,
      an exaggeration for the sake of making a point,
      not a statement of fact.

I know I should give and be and do all for You, Lord,
     but I simply haven't got that far as yet;
     perhaps one day I might.
     I know I ought to,
     but still . . .
     You see . . .

# Empty!

FOLK SAID IT WAS A GOOD TALK, MASTER;
thoughts running freely, words chosen with care,
but as I took my seat I heard Your silent verdict:
     'Empty!'


I don't want to be an empty can, Lord.
I don't want to be a show-case filled with duds.
     I want to be real, through and through;
not only real myself, but filled with Your presence,
     transmitting Your love and Your life.


O frightening emptiness . . .
     a hollow soul,
     just a shell!
     Save me from that, Master.

Of course it might have been the Tempter's whisper.
He's always trying to spike my guns,
to destroy my defences from within,
      old Quisling that he is.
You must forgive me, Lord, if I say that I can hardly tell
      the difference between Your voice and his.
He's a masterhand at imitation.
If I could be sure it was him talking I wouldn't care.
But I have a feeling, a strong feeling, that it was You.
And before the verdict from Your lips of 'Empty!' I quail.

      I don't want to be a vacuum, Master!
      Fill me, fill me with Your spirit
      so that I have something to give,
      something direct from You –
      a live transmission.

# Tired of being unselfish

I'M TIRED OF BEING UNSELFISH, MASTER;
tired of taking the burnt toast,
      the cracked cup,
      the squashed tomato,
      the broken fish,
      the bruised banana,
      the smallest egg
      and so on.

It doesn't make me any less selfish either,
for I get a kick out of 'denying myself',
hearing silent applause of me by me
        in the back of my mind.

And out of the corner of my eye I see 'Saint in Embryo'
        fingering his halo,
        eager to don it at the slightest encouragement,
        thrilled to have a part to play.

So I'm tired of being unselfish, Lord,
tired of being compulsively unselfish, that is;
        urging myself from within,
        always working against the grain,
        and ever forcing the issue.

I want something better, something higher, something
        nobler,
something that only You can give me.
        I want a love for others
        that will make me want to give them the best;
        that their good shall be my delight
        and their joy my reward.

Is it too much to ask of You, Master,
this outgoing love that will make me forget myself,
so that I no longer think of 'denying myself'
(Self is happy to parade even under that banner)?
A positive love, not a negative restraint . . .
Lord, in Your rich mercy will You grant me this?

# Things possess me

LORD, I'VE MADE A DISAPPOINTING DISCOVERY.
 Things possess me:
I'd always tried to believe that I was the ascetic type;
 not the real ascetic, of course,
 facts were against that,
 but with tendencies in that direction.
Now I find that what is mine is very important to me,
 even if it is not of any great worth.


It must be Great-aunt Maria behind this, Lord,
for she was a miser if ever there was one.
 Bits of old string,
 paper bags,
 empty boxes and bottles . . .
Those were some of her more harmless acquisitions,
and I find that I can't throw them away without wincing.


I don't want to be bound by things, Lord;
 to use, yes;
 to enjoy, yes;
 to lend, sometimes;
 but to hoard,
 simply to gloat over their possession, no!

Your Book tells us a few home-truths, Master.
It reminds us that even as we brought nothing into this
       world,
so we depart, empty-handed.
It makes one think.

There must be some secret formula to follow,
      to hold in trust,
      to use wisely,
      to treasure unpossessively
      and be ready to surrender.

I have a lot to learn, Lord;
please teach me how to sit lightly to this world's goods.

# Your love is stern

YOUR LOVE IS STERN, LORD,
steel-centred and unyielding.
It envelops me gently but it challenges me straitly.
There is no soft sentimentality about it;
      no fond blindness to faults,
      no condoning of disobedience,
      no deafness to disloyalty
      or minimising of wrong-doing.

You are not like an indulgent father who says:
      'Never mind what the children do,
      as long as they enjoy themselves'.

Your purpose is not my enjoyment
      but my development;
      my development in Christian character.

You set tests and tasks to be performed.
      You discipline, and demand results.
      You pull, push and prick
      until I fain would cry out:
        'Enough. Leave me.'

But You won't leave me, will You, Master?
      Even when I am most rebellious,
      when I writhe and squirm,
      when I protest most loudly,
for it is then that I most need You, Lord.

Your love is stern, Master,
      but I would not have it otherwise.
      You have set Yourself a hard task,
      trying to make a sinner into a saint.

# That awful record

THERE'S AN AWFUL RECORD PLAYING, LORD,
    Playing all the time.
I can't get away from it,
I can't deafen my ears to it,
    for it's in my own mind, Master.

Now You made my mind and You know its workings.
It's a fine piece of mechanism which You have created.
Why then should it play over and over again silly incidents
    which I
    want to forget?
    Over and over, Lord,
    until in irritation I say: 'Shut up'.

But my mind won't shut up, Lord.
It goes on churning over the same old grievances, the
    same
    old petty grudges,
    and I don't like it.

You made my mind, Master.
But I suppose that I must accept responsibility for what
    I have put into it.
Certain things have made deep grooves and the needle
    sticks,
    just there, and there . . .

Lord, I'd like to break that old mental record;
    smash it,
    throw it out,
    be free from it.
But how can I, when it is in my own brain?

Is it possible that part of me enjoys its self-pitying
      meanderings
and that is why I can't get rid of it?
Master, will You show me how I can deal with this enemy
      entrenched within me?

# WITH CLEARER SIGHT

# Make me realistic

MAKE ME REALISTIC, MASTER.
Let me define terms to myself.
I know I need a greater love for souls,
but what are 'souls', Lord?

Help me not to think of them as
        feather-light, clinic-clean wraiths
        floating invisibly around;
        interesting because unidentified,
        lovable because unknown.

Help me to remember that 'souls' are just people:
        old bodies with smelly breath and irritating ways,
        youngsters decked out in long hair and tight pants,
        children with runny noses and grimy fingernails,
        rich old ladies nursing lapdogs, and many others.

Keep me, Lord from praying for souls in general
        while ignoring my nearest neighbour.

Don't let me kid myself that I love souls
        when I can't stand the sight of Mrs. Smith.
        Mrs. Smith is a soul,
        doubtless a very skinny, under-nourished one,
Squeezed almost out of existence by a fat, over-nourished
        body,
        but nevertheless a soul, a needy soul.


Make me realistic, Lord.
Open my eyes to the fact that love for souls is simply
        caring about people.
It's harder put like that, Master.
        Souls are comfortably distant and abstract;
        people are uncomfortably near and substantial.
It's almost a pity that I see it so clearly now,
for I'll have to do something about it.
I'll try. I really will, I promise You, Lord.




# A glad spendthrift


I WANT TO BE A SPENDTHRIFT, LORD,
        a spendthrift of my time and strength,
        giving instead of withholding,
        sowing instead of wanting to reap.

Don't let me be a miser, Master,
     cuddling myself to myself,
     careful of every effort,
     counting each step,
     hoarding my physical resources
For the demands of a tomorrow that might never come.

Make me a glad spendthrift, Lord:
     joyously giving my love and care,
     opening the sluice-gates of my small reserves,
     pouring out what little I have to give
     without measure or stint,
     without anxious debate,
     and trusting You for tomorrow.

Don't let me shelter myself in a glass case,
     fearful lest the light of day should fade me,
     dreading that the hand of time should touch me,
     shrinking from effort that might drain me,
     saving myself up . . . for what?
     To look nice in my coffin?

Let me give what I have to give with open hands,
offering myself to You each day for service,
happy to be used as long as life shall last,
living for You as a glad spendthrift.
     For at the end, Lord,
     You will not ask me what I have saved,
     but what I have given.

# A good programme

I HAD SWITCHED OFF,
not knowing it was coming;
so I lost a treat,
something that would have brought me joy,
moments wonderful to experience
and enriching to remember;
but I had switched off.

That happens, too, Lord, when You speak to me.
I don't always hear
because I don't always listen.
I have switched off my spiritual receiver.

And times of enrichment pass me by
leaving me unmoved, unchanged.
I have no one to blame,
the fault is my own.
I wasn't receptive to You just then,
and my life is impoverished,
just that bit poorer,
because I wasn't listening.
I had switched off.

Help me to keep my heart open to You, Lord,
my spirit receptive,
my soul at its listening post.

For You have much to say to me,
things that I need to know,
words for my strengthening,
guidance for my way.

Keep me tuned in, Master, listening, waiting,
eager to receive;
and ready to act on
all that You have to say to me.

# Those aggressive posters

IT'S NOT LIKE IN YOUR DAYS, MASTER.
The streets of Nazareth were not plastered with advertise-
ments.
Loud, aggressive posters.
Subtle, persuasive posters –
buy this;
use that;
drink the other.

It stimulates the appetite, Lord.
It creates a want,
a need,
an urge,

to possess,
to be with it,
to live on a level with the Joneses.

Life is complex in our days, Master.
Shall we walk with eyes averted
studying the paving stones,
the bits of rubbish in the gutter?
Or shall we walk with upturned gaze
peering at the clouds chased by the wind?

What other solution is there?
To learn to say 'No' to these enticements?
But 'No' is a hard word.
Hard to say, but harder still to mean.
Your servant Paul said he had learnt to be content with
what he had,
which wasn't very much at times.
Perhaps You would help me to learn that lesson too,
and thus save me from falling into snares set by skilful
salesmen.

# The simple life

I'M ALL FOR THE SIMPLE LIFE, LORD.
    Just a toothbrush and towel,
    a handkerchief and comb,
    a change of clothes and shoes.


Few possessions, few demands, few worries.
What freedom of spirit when one is not cluttered with
        things!
What joy in renouncing the chains others forge for them-
        selves!
What delight in simple pleasures:
    the flight of a bird,
    the scent of a rose,
    the soft patter of rain!


What are possessions but ties that bind one to earth,
cords that hamper the soul's free movement?
All this I know and feel, Lord.
But there is one word which upsets my equanimity.
    It is a little word,
    but it is powerful, Master,
    and it occurs so often;
    just four letters
    S-A-L-E.

What magical magnet is hidden in those letters?
The attraction of the simple life fades,
     the joys of the simple life vanish.
I am caught, impaled, tempted beyond my strength,
and I acquire things
     because they appear cheap,
     because they are enticingly presented,
     and skilfully advertised.
Lord, can You deliver me from sale fever?


# The ant-heap


I THOUGHT OF YOU, LORD, WHEN I SAW THAT
     ANT-HEAP.
I stood watching it, fascinated by its ceaseless bustle.
     An ant-city three feet in diameter,
     an ant-world complete in itself.
Narrow paths radiated at angles into the forest,
paths tramped bare by millions of tiny ant-feet,
as great an adventure for them as our space-probes.

I thought of You watching our world,
     our comings and goings,
     our endless activity,
     all centred on one cramped blob in space,
     a small rotating orb.

What are Your thoughts as You observe us?
>Knowing the immensity of the universe,
>do You pity us packed together so tightly
>on our little ball,
>hurrying, scurrying,
>fretting our hearts out
>if it rains on washing day,
>or the train is late?


O God, save us from thinking that this brief life is all.
Give us a glimpse of the vastness of eternity,
>of a coming life as far exceeding this one
>as that of an ant transformed to man.


>When the shackles of time are broken,
>when the body releases its grip on the soul,
then, then, we shall know for the first time
>what it is to live,
>really live.



# Unfinished things


TODAY, LORD, I SEE MY LIFE LIKE A HIGHWAY,
I look back and, as far as memory can trace,
I see unfinished things thrown aside.

I have been a veritable litter-bug in this respect.
> The thrill of starting something fresh;
> the enthusiasm for a new idea;
> the joy of creating;
> then the slackening of interest as the new venture
>> palled.
> Laying it aside;
> forgetting it for many days:
> and finally throwing it away.

It's not wrong, Lord, to have thrown so much aside.
The fault was in beginning too much.
> As a child it is good to try one's skills;
> but adults must discriminate.

If I accept this, I must relinquish that;
if I give time to this, I must sacrifice that;
if I choose this, I must renounce that.

> I need wisdom, Master.
> I need Your help, Your guidance.
For I have only one life to live,
only so much time invested in the bank of life,
and I want my life to count.

> To count for good;
> to accomplish something useful;
> to help bring in Your Kingdom.

Show me, then, what things are worth while, Lord,
and help me do them with all my heart and mind.

# Weeds and flowers

THERE IS ONE THING I SHOULD LIKE TO ASK YOU,
    LORD.
        It has puzzled me often:
why do weeds grow easier than flowers?

I see it right before my eyes:
        I sow flowers and produce weeds.
        I sow grass and raise nettles;
my frail plants are choked by luscious dandelions.

Now I have no personal animosity against dandelions,
    Master.
        They are bright, jolly flowers.
        Sensible too,
        for they shut up at night,
        which is more than many people do,
        judging by the noise one hears.

But why should dandelions that I don't plant
        thrive better than the flowers I protect?
How is it that from a packet of choice seeds
        I raise chickweed?

If it were only a question of flowers and weeds
        it would be strange enough,

but the tendency goes further and deeper.
 I find it within my own being,
 a downward pull,
 a gravitation to a lower level.

It is a daily fight to keep the standard high,
 to bring forth flowers instead of weeds,
 good instead of evil
 in my life, character and service.

Lord, is it a law in Your moral world,
 as well as in Your natural world,
that the more valuable the product
 the harder it is to produce?


# Leisure

LEISURE IS FRIGHTENING, MASTER:
 a string of empty hours,
 a missing day in the almanac,
 a blank page in life's book.
The stream of time slipping unnoticed through careless
  fingers;
 nothing thought,
 nothing experienced,
 nothing achieved.

A long road leading nowhere, sprouting useless cul-de-
        sacs;
    no direction,
    no purpose,
    no goal.

Help me to use leisure wisely, Lord,
    to enjoy Your beautiful world,
    to learn more of Your marvellous creation;
    to enrich my mind,
    to water friendship's garden.

For one day I shall have to give account
    to none other than to You, Lord,
    how I have used the gift of time.
    Time to work, to rest, to play,
    time to serve others and enjoy others.

You will ask me not only what I have done,
    but what I have left undone.

Help me then not to waste one single moment.
    And when no taskmaster stands over me,
    when I am left to my own devices,
    let me use leisure wisely,
    knowing for that too
    You will hold me to account.

# Forgive Your world

DON'T TIRE OF YOUR WORLD, MASTER.
Don't wash Your hands of Your children,
      shaking us off as hopeless,
      worthless.
      Give us one more chance,
      and yet another,
      and another.

How Your heart must sorrow as You see our need;
      our selfishness and sinfulness,
      cruelty and degradation,
      indifference to Your commands,
      contempt of Your love.

If our hearts sicken over the daily news,
      what must You feel?
You who hold the world in Your cupped hands,
      bending over it lovingly;
      listening, yearning,
      challenging to better ways.

Yet spiteful arrows pierce Your heart daily;
Your malicious children spit up in Your face:
that kind face bent over them in tender compassion.

Father-God, forgive Your world:
go on forgiving Your children.
>    Don't leave us to our own devices,
>    to our self-made hell,
>    don't cast us away,
flinging us like unwanted playthings into the chill of
>    outer space.

We have no merits to plead;
our very wickedness must speak for us.
We need You.

O God, forgive Your world:
give us one more chance.

# LISTEN, LORD

# A living contact

LORD, I WANT TO BE A LIVING CONTACT FOR YOU,
      a link between You and other people.
I've known You for so many years now,
        that I can recommend You to others who need you.


People do need You, Master, but they don't realise it.
They want to be happy and loved,
        to find a meaning to life.


They don't understand that only when lived with You
        can life find its truest expression.


They carry a hidden burden of conscience-distress
        and fail to see that only You can forgive sin
        and lift the load from them.


They complain of boredom and frustration, not knowing
        that You can add an extra dimension to their lives.

They are dissatisfied and unhappy, not realising that You
    can provide the missing ingredient.


So that is why, Lord, I want to be a living contact for You.
I want to tell people what You have done for me and
    others.


Sometimes I feel that I'd like to stand in the market-places
    of the world
    and shout aloud for all to hear;
    crying not my own wares, but Yours.


Help me, Master, in my own way and just where I am,
    to be a living contact for You,
    a link between You and other people.
    For they do need You.


# Someone to listen


MASTER, THE WORLD IS IN A HURRY,
    from morning till night,
    working, running, talking,
    busy with a thousand things.
No one has time to listen to me,
and I need to talk.

I have so much to say.
Not only small talk about everyday affairs,
     but about deeper things.
I need time to explain how I feel within me,
     the strange longings,
     the disturbing doubts,
     the questionings and probings,
     the hurts I suffer.


I don't only live on the surface, Lord.
There's a lot going on behind my quiet mien.
     Things hard to speak about,
     unless someone will listen,
     really listen to me.
     But no one has time.


So it is all bottled up within my breast,
until at times I feel that I shall burst
     with the inward pressure.


Can I talk to You, Master?
Will You listen patiently
     if my words falter at times,
     if I find it hard to explain myself?
It will bring such relief if I can pour it all out to You,
     for You understand.
With a whole universe to govern,
You have yet time for each single soul.

Thank You, Lord!
I'm sitting at Your feet now,
and You are listening,
so I begin my tale . . .

# Peace

HOW COULD YOU, LORD, SPEAK OF INWARD PEACE
when the snares of wicked men were closing round You
and a stark Cross loomed ahead?

From what hidden spring did You drink?
What inward resources gave You Your strength?
    I'd like to know Your secret, Lord,
    for I, too, need Your peace.

Not the stillness of a graveyard, a dead peace;
not cloistered serenity, the peace of withdrawal;
not the calm that narcotics give, a doped peace;
it's Your peace I want, Master.

The peace of a clear conscience,
    of a disciplined life,
    an integrated character.
The peace of vigorous action in a righteous cause,
    a vibrant, joyous peace.

You spoke of peace as a gift, Lord.
Can anyone receive it from You?
Can I? In spite of my frustrations,
      in spite of my anxieties,
      in spite of my failures?

Dare I ask You for it?
Just now, Lord?
Yes, just now.

# Noise

No transistor broke the silence of your
    galilean hills, Master.
    When You left the crowded village
    and sought the stillness of the heights,
    you could hear the twitter of birds,
    the hum of insects,
    the soft swish of the wind through tufted grass,
    and in the silence God could speak to You.

But I live in days of tension, of speed, of noise.
My generation is afraid of silence,
afraid of listening, in case they hear . . . nothing.

We are keyed up to noise, drowned in canned music,
persistent voices pursuing us the round of the clock.
Is it any wonder that we are tense and nervy?

In Your Book the seer tells of silence in heaven
    for what seemed half an hour.
    Blest break in the celestial chanting,
    welcome pause in the heavenly harmonies:
    A whole half hour . . .
    deep, satisfying silence,
    something to look forward to
    when earthly noise grates harshly on the ear.

In the meantime, Lord, help me to draw within myself,
    stilling myself in the silence of my soul;
    there finding strength and refreshing,
    shut off from the world's jarring noises
    for a few brief moments at a time.
    A quiet oasis in a desert of sound.
    There in that silence
    I shall meet with You
    and again be strong.


# Only one


LORD, YOU HAVE PROMISED TO BE WHERE TWO OR
    THREE MEET.
That thought has been an inspiration to many.
But I am neither two nor three,
    I am only one.
    Is Your promise for me too?

I remember Nicodemus coming to You at night,
  creeping stealthily up the steps
  to find You alone.
  To him You opened Your heart,
  and he went out into the dark a changed man.

I remember the woman at the well.
  You asked her for a drink.
  It was a kindly way of making contact.
  And then You spoke to her,
  showed what her life had been
  and what it could be;
  that day she would never forget.

So I take courage:
though I am alone, I do not need to feel lonely,
  to brood over the stings of life,
  to consume my own smoke
  or to bear alone a weight of sorrow.

I, too, can meet with You. I can share with You,
share my secret hopes and fears,
  talk out my distresses,
  ventilate my problems,
  and know that You understand
  and love me.

# I can't pray

Y OUR SERVANT THE APOSTLE, L ORD, TOLD US
ALWAYS TO PRAY,
but I can't . . .
I simply can't.
I'm not made that way.
My mind wanders,
my foot twitches,
and I remember, Lord.

Remember that I have to fetch the washing in,
that I promised to phone Mrs. Farley,
that I forgot to buy flour yesterday,
and many other things.
Many, many other things.
So You understand, Master, that it is difficult for me to
pray.

Would You mind if I just chatted to You about everything
while it is happening?
In that way, Lord, I could keep in contact with You.

I could tell You of the things that worry me,
the things that puzzle me,
the things I detest
and the things I enjoy.

And my longings, Master, the deep, deep longings,
    that You Yourself have planted in my heart.


It may not be the highest kind of prayer,
it may not be what others can offer You,
    but it will be my way of praying,
    and I believe that You will understand
    and accept it.


# Do You listen?


DO YOU LISTEN, MASTER, WHEN PEOPLE PRAY?
Do You hear what they say to You?
    Every single voice that rises
    from the four corners of the earth
    in infinite tongues
    at all hours of the day and night,
    do You listen to it all?


Did You catch the wonderful phrase in that man's prayer
    today?
    He addressed You as: 'O effulgent Majesty'.
    Do You like to be called 'effulgent Majesty'?
    Then he told You the news of the day:
    was it news to You?

Sometimes, Lord, a very sobering thought strikes me,
that You don't listen at all to what people are saying
    in their very long and wordy prayers,
    filled with well-oiled, rolling phrases,
    all of a pattern as it was in the beginning.

I'm almost afraid to follow my thought out to its natural
      sequence.
For, Master, if You don't listen to our words,
    but only read our hearts and minds,
    our hidden longings and desires,
    then what we say and what we pray
    might be poles apart.
    And that thought makes me tremble.

When did I last pray to You, really pray,
my stumbling words the imperfect vehicle of my soul's
      searching,
    my silence the awe of worship in Your presence?
    Lord, I have need of You just now.
    Teach me to pray,
    truly pray.

# LEARNING IN GOD'S
## SCHOOL

# A dunce in Your school

LORD, I'VE MUFFED IT AGAIN!
I'm just a dunce in Your school.
      I knew I had failed,
      and You knew it too,
      but You said nothing.
Have patience with me!
I'm always going over the same old lessons
and never really learning them.

I was so sure I could handle that situation.
      I've had plenty of experience of it
      and through trial and error have learnt what not to
        do,
      so I had the theory all right.

I'm sure that if you tested me in theory only
      I could make a better showing.
      But You are not satisfied with theory.
      You insist upon practice,
      and that is where I fail.

Why, Lord, should there be such a gulf fixed
      between theory and practice?
      To know what to do
      and yet not do it;
      to see the pitfalls
      and yet stumble into them?

Do You tire of having such a poor pupil,
and feel like washing Your hands of me?
      Give me another chance!
Perhaps You can show me a better way to learn my lessons,
      so that I don't fail so often.
I want to learn, I really do.
I'm beginning to see that the secret is
      to keep in close touch with You,
      rather than to rely on theoretical knowledge
      or my own endeavours.

Teach me then, Master, so that I can make some progress;
I don't want to stay for ever the dunce in Your school.

# Half-truths

HOW DO YOU REGARD HALF-TRUTHS, MASTER?
In Your reckoning do two half-truths equal a whole truth,
    or do they add up to one big, whopping lie?
    I hope the former,
    but I fear the latter;
    and my fear is greater than my hope.
Can truth be halved or quartered?
Can it be coloured, shaded or distorted?
    Or is it immutable, inviolable?


Your Book reminds me that You are truth,
    and that knowledge makes me wary of You,
    for You know all,
In Your presence my cleverest subtleties fail to register,
    my rationalisations are transparent,
    my self-deceptions dissolve;
And I stand revealed, unprotected, in the blazing light
    of Your absolute truth.


Lord, is it possible for me to be completely truthful,
To balance my words on the hair-spring of absolute
       truth,
to think without my thought being tinted by my fears or
       desires,

not to deviate from the plumbline of truth
    by a glance,
    a tone of voice,
    a shrug of the shoulders,
    a calculated emphasis,
    a nod of approval,
    a sniff of disdain,
    a lengthened pause . . .?


Master, grant me sincerity! Make me truthful.
Let your light search me as I can bear it,
    and so prepare me for the day
    when I shall be exposed to all its intensity.


# A mixed bunch

WHAT MADE YOU DECIDE ON YOUR TWELVE DIS-
    CIPLES, MASTER?
They were rather a mixed bunch when You took them in
    hand,
if You don't mind my saying so.
    Hot-tempered zealots,
    ambitious place-seekers,
    rough-worded fishermen,
    and just ordinary folk.

But they turned out well, all but one,
      and that was not Your fault
      for You tried to save him.

When I look around at Your followers of today,
      we, too, seem rather a mixed bunch.
Some stand out like giants among their fellows,
      but the rest of us are very ordinary.
You seem to have a flair for picking out unlikely indivi-
      duals
      and finding a use for them.

Why, Lord, did You call me to follow You?
What a lot of trouble You would have saved Yourself
      if You'd let me go my own way.
Did You really want me in Your following
or were You trying to save me from myself?

Thank You a thousand times for that beckoning finger
      and the impulse You gave me to respond.
      I wish I'd been more loyal to Your leadership,
      profited more from Your teaching
      and been a better representative of Yours.

But I do thank You, for You filled my life with meaning;
      You gave me a settled purpose,
      broadened and deepened my thinking,
and helped me to meet life's storms with a steady keel.
      So thank You, Master.
From the depths of my heart, thank You.

# Kind to the unthankful

LORD, YOUR BOOK SAYS THAT YOU ARE KIND TO
THE UNTHANKFUL.
I'm not like that, Master.
I'm kind until people prove unthankful,
and then I feel like leaving them to it,
washing my hands of them.

But You go on being kind,
even against anger and hate,
scorn and cold indifference,
wooing with love the hardened hearts of men.

Why do You do it, Lord?
Do You spy the glint of gold among the rubble?
Can You see the makings of a man in a ne'er-do-well?
Or sense the texture of fine womanhood in a slut?
Or can You do it just because You are You?
Because You really do care about people,
really love them in spite of their nastiness?

I think that must be the secret,
and that is why I react differently.
You pour out love in such abundance,
that it sweeps around and over all obstacles.
You love because it is Your nature to love,
without thought of recompense or return.

Is love like that something one can learn, Master?
> Or has it to be a gift,
> a gift from You?
> If so, will You grant it me,
> in the measure that I can contain it?

# Side tracks

THE PICTURE DID NOT TELL THE WHOLE STORY,
> LORD.
> I remember it clearly
for it made a great impression on my childish mind,
the narrow gate leading through many adventures to life,
the broad gate leading straight to the fires of hell.
> It was a sermon in itself,
> harsh and vivid,
> frightening to a young mind.

To my mature mind it seems that the artist had got one
> thing wrong.
> He didn't show the side tracks.

He depicted two distinct roads each governed by its
> entrance.
Experience has taught me that many are the side tracks
> that lead from the narrow path to the broad:

111

the way of compromise,
the way of ease,
the way of lowered ideals,
neglect of the means of grace,
and many others.

Lord, these side tracks are not clearly marked.
They open so easily, so pleasantly, so conveniently;
they follow parallel for a time,
and their final destination is hidden.

How am I to know which is the true narrow path,
and which the false side track,
when they look so alike?

Master, I have passed through the narrow door at Your
call,
and I am trying to keep on the right road.
At each fork will You help me to choose aright,
for I want to follow the Way of Life,
which leads to Your heavenly mansions?

# Quite an adventure

I'VE HAD QUITE AN ADVENTURE, MASTER.
I've wandered through the bowels of London all alone.
    All alone, that is,
    with hundreds of thousands of other people.
    Jostling, shoving, running,
    up and down passages, escalators, stairs.

For one thing is certain in these days, Lord.
    Everyone is going somewhere;
    no one is content to stay put.

And I was going somewhere.
    So I descended the stairs,
    was propelled down escalators,
    squeezed into steamy tube trains,
    changing here, changing there.

Northbound? Southbound?
How could I judge the points of the compass in London's
    intestines?

Then I saw a light with a magic word printed across it.
    I followed the light up hill and down dale,
    and came to my journey's end.

Life is bewildering, Lord.
People are going in all directions.
　　　How shall I find my course?
Follow the light, You say?
　　　I will, Master.


But please let it shine extra bright at awkward corners,
　　　for I am apt to stumble
　　　and go astray.


# A distorted picture

YOU MUST FORGIVE US, MASTER.
We mean well when we talk so much of Your love
　　　and soft-pedal Your anger;
but we are giving a distorted picture,
　　　a wrong image,
　　　a one-sided view of You.


We avoid the issue by omitting to read
　　　Your scornful words on subterfuge,
　　　Your hatred of hypocrisy,
　　　Your blazing anger against injustices,
　　　Your sharp words to tricksters.

You lashed out against the religious humbugs of Your day;
    'play actors' You called them,
    'hypocrites' You hurled at them,
    'blind leaders of the blind',
    'brood of vipers' . . .
    You did not spare hard words.

You couldn't expect to be popular when You used such
    language.
    You cut across vested interests,
    You stirred up hatred,
    You created enemies,
    and You paid the penalty with Your life.
Help us, Lord, to remember Your anger against deceit.
    Don't let us imagine we can double-cross You,
    pretending to be what we are not,
    or think that we can sow without reaping.

Lord, You are flaming justice as well as tender love;
give us a wholesome fear of Your condemnation.

# Incredible!

IT'S INCREDIBLE, MASTER,
beyond all understanding
that You should be willing to identify Yourself with the
    human race.
What is there to commend us?

You know the whole long story of our vicious passions,
   so I don't need to elaborate;
and You chose to become one with us,
to be born of lowly parentage in a cattle shed.
   Incredible!

It might be argued that You didn't know just how bad
   we were before You came,
but You certainly soon found out.
Yet Your favourite name for Yourself was Son of Man.
Weren't You ashamed openly to link Yourself with
   humans,
   knowing us as we are?
Yet You did it, and did it willingly.

Sometimes I get a glimpse of what it must have cost You,
   this humiliation,
   this self-imposed limitation,
   coming down to our level –
You, the source of all life, limited in movement and power;
You, immortal and eternal, binding Yourself with the
   chains of time;
You, the mighty ocean, willing to live as a single droplet;
You, Lord of all, becoming a village carpenter;
You, the sinless One, dying for our sins.
   Incredible, yet true!

Thank you, Lord, because You did it,
   for my sake,
   for all of us,
   Thank You!

# This fellow

YOU HAD MANY TAUNTS FLUNG AT YOU, MASTER,
     as You trod this earth of ours.
Insults, scorn and hatred flourished round You,
     but perhaps the most barbed of all
     were the contemptuous words:
'This fellow welcomes bad people and eats with them.'

It was intended as a smack in the face for You, Lord.
     You went to parties and weddings,
     as well as to sick-beds and funerals.
     At one time You were quite popular
     and even sought after,
but You were not very discriminating
     in the type of folk You mixed with,
     so they thought You didn't know.

Didn't know that rich clothing hid a grasping, selfish
       heart,
that flowing robes concealed a harlot's body;
that compliments were but the grappling irons of a trap,
     a trap to catch You,
     and kill You.

As though You didn't know . . .
You with the steady eyes that saw through people,

with the keen perception that weighed motives
and quickly summed up character.

You gave them an answer:
what was meant as a gibe, You took as a compliment.
     You put Your cards on the table
     and told them straight out:
'I'm not looking for good people, but for bad.'
They hated You all the more for that remark,
     for it baffled them.

But it gives us courage to come to You, Master.
We know that You welcome such as we are.
You welcome crooked characters to put them straight,
You welcome the sick at heart to make them well,
You welcome sinners to make them saints.
You welcome me. For that I thank You.

# UNKNOWN
# TOMORROWS

# The great beyond

I WISH YOU HAD TOLD US MORE ABOUT THE GREAT
      BEYOND, LORD.
    We're all heading there
    whether we like it or not.
    By air, rail, road, sea,
    or on plain Shanks's pony,
    we're all on our way into the Unknown.


It's not easy for our western minds to understand You
    when You talk in picture language.
    You must forgive our denseness
    and our terrible literal-mindedness.


Your servant Paul told of being snatched up to the third
    heaven.
Was that just a phrase he used to indicate highest bliss,
as we speak today of being in the seventh heaven?
Or are there really stages in the Beyond?

Is the third heaven the tourist class, so to speak,
with possibility of rising to first class?
Or is the third heaven the utmost pinnacle of joy?

To be quite frank with You, Master,
    I feel a bit scared at times.
    Not of You, but of the Unknown.

I am comforted when I think of the repentant thief,
    dying on the cross next to Yours.
    When he turned to You in his utter need,
    You promised that he should be with You
    in Paradise.

Where is Paradise? What is Paradise?
    Is it the forecourt of heaven,
    or heaven itself?

I don't know. But the operative thought is 'with You'.
    So when I feel afraid, I comfort myself . . .
    I shall be with You
    and all will be well.

# A human caterpillar

I'M JUST A CATERPILLAR, MASTER,
    earthbound and clumsy,
    heavy feet hugging the ground;
    a crawler,
    eyes glued to a cabbage leaf.
    Slow, painfully slow in progress.
Limited activity, limited vision, limited horizon.

But, in my heart, my caterpillar-heart, I dream . . .
dream of the day when I shall shed my cumbrous
    clothing,
    say good-bye to my clodfootedness,
    rise from my chrysalis-coffin,
and on flashing wings skim the eternities of the upper
    sphere.

    Free! free at last,
    free of my former fetters,
    denizen of another world.
'This perishable thing clothed with the imperishable,
this mortal clothed with immortality.'
    O great, glad day!
    O hope within my soul,
    O glorious promise,
    destiny divine!

But just now, Lord, I'm still at the crawling stage,
    earthbound and clumsy,
    heavy feet hugging the ground,
    slow, painfully slow in progress.


In Your goodness grant me this favour, dear Lord;
let not my sluggish gait rob me of my vision.
    I shall rise
    clothed with immortality
    to join You in the Great Beyond!
It is Your own promise, Lord, and on that promise I rely.


# What is hell like?

MASTER, WHAT IS HELL REALLY LIKE?
I know of course that it is a state rather than a place,
but what is it like?
You spoke of hell in many terms, all of them symbolic,
but there must be some reality behind the word-pictures.


Is hell simply separation from You
    and from all goodness, love and beauty?
Is it the reverse side, the dark side, the cold side,
    the negation of all that makes our best selves?

Or is it truth, Lord? Stark, undiluted truth
    to which one is exposed,
    from which one can't run,
    there being nowhere to hide?
The impact of that moment must be terrible;
    inescapable, blazing truth,
frightful to face when one is filled with shams and lies;
    agony to endure its prolongation.

Sometimes I have thought that hell must be self-chosen;
    a flight into darkness,
    into horrible unending blackness,
    a shrinking back into deep shadows,
    a voluntary self-exclusion to escape the light;
    the penetrating light of Your presence,
    revealing all our inward defilement,
    purity which cannot tolerate evil.

One thing You have said, Master, in no mistaken terms,
    You have warned us of the horrors of hell,
    and You have provided an alternative.

# A guttering candle

A GUTTERING CANDLE IS NO PLEASANT SIGHT.
Had it tongue to speak, what might it say?

Look not on what I am now,
　　　but what I was.
　　　Tall, straight, shapely.
Bravely I shed my light on all around,
knowing that as I gave, I was myself consumed.

Harsh winds of life beat upon me,
　　　challenging my right to shine,
　　　fluttering my flame hither and thither.
　　　My strength dripped from me,
　　　yet I remained alight,
　　　faintly flickering.

Lord, this guttering candle speaks to me.
I, too, have known the pride of youth and strength,
held my head high and daily done my tasks.

But now the sun has passed its zenith,
strain and stress of duties have taken their toll,
winds of change have whirled around me,
　　　but by Your grace,
　　　my light still burns.

Grant me one favour, Master.
Let my light flicker until the end,
until my flame sinks spent
       into final rest.

# Tomorrow

TOMORROW IS AN X-DAY, LORD,
an unknown quantity of unknown quality.
I'm not even sure that there will be a tomorrow.
       It's a might-be, not a shall-be.
So far in my life sunrise has always followed sunset,
       but it won't always be so.

What does tomorrow conceal in its travelling bag?
       Joyous surprises?
       Let them all come.
       Good news?
       I'm thirsting for it.

Or there might possibly be sorrows . . .
       the death of a loved one?
If so, help me to be grateful for the hours we shared,
let memories bind a golden chain.
       Is sickness in the offing?
Let me learn lessons of patience and endurance.

Catastrophe may suddenly strike me:
    road accident?
    train wreck?
    air disaster?
    who knows?

Life has many ingredients, some good, some bad.
All kinds must come my way at some time.

Keep my heart steady, Lord, whatever tomorrow may
        bring.
Let me hold Your hand and walk unafraid with You;
for finally, Master, You will write one word
    over my earthly life,
    and that word will be
    FINIS.